Ohio's Monsters and Mysterious Beasts

ISBN-978-1-940087-64-1
Copyright © 2023
by Jannette Quackenbush

Let me help you find your scary place.

About the author: *Jannette Quackenbush is the author of 30 books, including Moonville: Its Past. Its Ghosts. Its Legends, Haunted Hiking Trails of the Appalachian Region, haunted Ohio, West Virginia, Pennsylvania, and New Orleans ghost guides. She is a veteran hiker, a seasoned backpacker, and a career author/naturalist/travel guide. She has provided tours and night hikes of Moonville and the surrounding communities. "I hike remote areas often throughout the Appalachians, 15 to 30 miles a week. I have found that the more you adventure in these rugged areas, the better your chances of seeing those mysterious wild things that others question exist."*

BackRoads Books
by 21 Crows
Jannette Quackenbush

Find Your Journey

Table of Contents

Bigfoot Creatures

Other Cryptids and Creatures

Williams, Fulton, Lucas, Ottawa, Defiance, Henry, Wood, Sandusky, Erie, Lorain, Cuyahoga, Lake, Ashtabula, Geauga, Trumbull, Paulding, Putnam, Hancock, Seneca, Huron, Medina, Summit, Portage, Mahoning, Van Wert, Allen, Wyandot, Crawford, Richland, Ashland, Wayne, Stark, Columbiana, Mercer, Auglaize, Hardin, Marion, Morrow, Holmes, Carroll, Harrison, Jefferson, Logan, Knox, Coshocton, Tuscarawas, Shelby, Union, Delaware, Darke, Champaign, Clark, Madison, Franklin, Licking, Muskingum, Guernsey, Belmont, Miami, Preble, Montgomery, Greene, Fayette, Pickaway, Fairfield, Perry, Morgan, Noble, Monroe, Washington, Butler, Warren, Clinton, Ross, Hocking, Athens, Hamilton, Clermont, Highland, Vinton, Meigs, Pike, Jackson, Gallia, Brown, Adams, Scioto, Lawrence

I've explored/researched the places in this book where these unique and mysterious creatures are found. I believe it is important that if I write about a subject, I have to research it, go to the site, see it for myself to be a reliable source. The small picture by each title is an image of the area as are most of the larger images. The images are my depictions of what others have described witnessing.

Salt Fork Bigfoot
Guernsey County

Salt Fork State Park has 17,229 acres for Bigfoot to inhabit, including many old, overgrown farmsteads and deep forests. It has all the ingredients of an ideal Bigfoot habitat: prey like deer, squirrels, and rabbits, plenty of room to roam, and water from Salt Fork Lake. It should not be surprising that there have been over 35 noted sightings since the late 1970s. Hikers and picnickers have heard deep howls and loud screams echoing through the valleys. Visitors have witnessed several of the creatures appear and found tracks after. And there are many more undocumented accounts that people have told me during the famous Ohio Bigfoot Conference held at Salt Fork over the years. Hikers and hunters have observed tall bipedal and hairy creatures in picnic areas, camping areas, trails, and the spillway.

In the summer of 2004, a couple picnicking were terrified when the man saw a nearly eight-foot-tall, dark-colored form looking at him and his wife. He was interviewed by the Daily Jeffersonian out of Cambridge, Ohio, and stated this: "What we saw —it was standing there. It was dark - I will not say it was covered with hair —but it was a dark figure standing nearly eight feet tall. I could see its head [move from side to side] like it is looking at me. And then it turns and keeps on walking [down the hill]."

A Bigfoot Along Rocky River
Cuyahoga County

Rocky River Reservation sprawls over 5600 acres in Cuyahoga County, centered along the Rocky River. It is known for its steep shale cliffs and deep valleys. It is filled with meadows, wetlands, and forests and is the perfect habitat for any wildlife with plenty of food and shelter. The river would allow an easy path for a large creature to follow.

In 2008, two women were fishing along the river about eight feet above the water along a rock wall when a herd of deer crossed the river. A few minutes passed when a towering black figure, taller than the average man, with a thick brow and long hair, emerged. The sunlight hit the creature's eyes, and they glowed red-orange. The women quickly snatched up their fishing gear and fled to their car.

The Hocking Hills Bigfoot
Hocking County

The Hocking Hills has millions of visitors a year. It seems unlikely that Bigfoot would want to tarry here for fear of being seen. However, nearby, Hocking State Forest, with its 9,815 acres and surrounding private properties, is where most sightings occur, mainly in the less-used forested area between Cedar Falls and Ash Cave. I live in the area and people often tell me, "Something's getting into my garbage again. It's too big for a coyote, bobcat, or bear, and it ain't no person."

Not too long ago, a hunter witnessed a seven-foot-tall ape-like creature covered with dark brown hair in the forested hunting area. This Bigfoot had a human-like nose, thick brow ridges, and a sloped forehead. In that same area, growls and deep yowls were heard. While filming for a project in the winter of 2023, I was alone, hiking the old forestry service road just past the gates, leaving Cedar Falls, and heading to Ash Cave. It was late afternoon when I heard a deep, guttural growl. Thinking it might have been a bear, I craned my neck to the left and looked up a steep hillside. I did not plan on pursuing something that might maul and eat me should my puny five-foot-something stature not terrify it. But as I homed in on it, it seemed to be a small ape squatting at the top. Feeling a bit cocky for my size and sure that I could disprove my eyes that it was nothing more than a rotting stump or a fat deer butt, I hurried up the hillside. Partway, as I lost my breath, the creature vanished. Although the brush was moved aside, no other evidence remained.

The Vinton County Grassman
Vinton County

Vinton County is one of Ohio's least populated, remote counties. It has many sightings of Bigfoot, called Grassman in parts of this region for the green moss growing on its coat, but fewer people report them to authorities. In small towns where everybody knows everybody, folks tend to shy away from being called, "It's that crazy one who said they saw a Bigfoot."

The history of Bigfoot sightings in Vinton County dates back to the 1880s, a time when the world was still unraveling its wild mysteries. However, after a 1950s witness account in Prattsville and the surge in sightings during the late summer and fall of 1980 near the county seat of McArthur, Vinton County's name became truly etched in Bigfoot history.

A monster mania pursued, and as the years passed, more witnesses came forward. One local described the Bigfoot: "It looked a lot like an ape. The darned thing was at least 10 feet tall, and it had real long arms. The odor it gave off was just awful. It was pungent . . . like maybe that creature hadn't had a bath in about a year." By May of 1988, a camo-clad and heavily armed party of hunters descended into McArthur's hills and valleys. They set up a military-style encampment with an armed posse to track this monster down. They did not find it and, thus, decided it was a hoax. But locals in Vinton County continue to have something bigger than a bear get into their garbage, curiously peer into their windows occasionally, and hap upon them in the isolated woodlands.

The Minerva Monster
Stark/Columbiana County

In the summer of 1978, the Herbert and Evelyn Cayton family of Minerva unwittingly disturbed a secret when clearing the undergrowth around their home. A colossal creature, its fur matted and its stature towering over six feet, began to make its presence known near an old strip mine behind their house. Whether the family was gathered on their porch with friends or huddled inside their home, they would catch sight of two sets of eyes, large and luminous, piercing the darkness with an otherworldly glow. The shadowy form would wander around the house, toss stones at the windows, and howl out in the black of night.

The family called the Stark County Sheriff's Department. Captain Jim Shannon arrived on the scene and scouted out the area. He immediately smelled an ammonia-sulfur scent. Later, the stories made it to the newspapers, and the family took a certain amount of mockery for what they saw even though there were multiple eye-witnesses of the account. The police, reporters, and the curious ventured from all over to search out The Minerva Monster. Nobody found it. And eventually, the story faded away.

But not so for the Minerva Monster. Sometimes, folks at the nearby trailer park catch a glimpse of it on the road or hear the rocks pelt the siding of their mobile homes. "Whatever it is, it's not dangerous," Evelyn Cayton would later tell Barbara Mudak, a staff writer with The Akron Beacon Journal. "If it was going to hurt someone, it would have done it by now."

Cedar Bog Monster
Champaign County

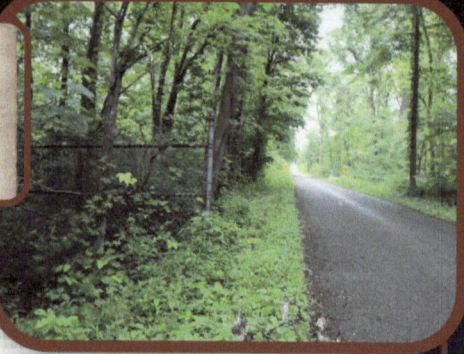

In 1942, the Ohio Historical Society listed Cedar Bog, near Urbana, as a nature preserve. It is not technically a bog because bogs do not drain; they are more like a swimming pool holding water. It is a fen because Cedar Bog drains into Cedar Run instead of holding water to evaporate, which is typical of this type of wetland. An example of a boreal and prairie fen, it is home to plenty of Ohio's rare plants and animals. It also has a cryptid lurking around in this nature preserve. Quite a few people have seen it. Not long after the historical society designated it as a preserve, witnesses saw a white hairy ape-like creature lurking along Woodburn Road near the fen. There were sightings by a couple using the old road beside Cedar Bog as a lover's lane. They witnessed an enormous, white creature staring in the car window at them. It made no noise, but it stank. There is a legend about the fence surrounding Cedar Bog. Rumors tell that a government agency placed a high chain-link fence around the fen. It was not to keep people out. Instead, they set it there to keep the monster within!

Orange-eye Sewer Monster Of Charles Mill Lake Richland/Ashland County

An algae-covered ape-like being with glowing orange eyes called the Orange Eye Sewer Monster stalks the area around Charles Mill Lake. Its existence is explained as this: It emerged from a tunnel beneath Riverside Cemetery in Cleveland after roadway construction workers inadvertently destroyed its home. The beast made its path to Charles Mill Lake, where it inhabits the shallower boggy areas. Sketchy reports from 1963 and 1968 (when children chased it with flashlights while playing) offered that the creature weighed at least 1000 pounds and was eleven feet tall with a matted coat covered in a fungal crust and dripping with green algae.

Green-eyed Monster Of Charles Mill Lake
Richland/Ashland County

Charles Mill Lake is a reservoir located in central Ohio, less than eight miles from Mansfield, constructed by damming the Black Fork of the Mohican River in 1935. On March 26th, 1959, three bored teen boys took off from their Mansfield homes and drove to Charles Mill Lake during a heavy fog. The boys drove down the lane behind the boathouse. They parked the car and sat there, staring out into the dark and water. A log in the water caught their attention; it moved and stood erect. "Our hair was standing on end," one boy told reporters later. "The Thing stood up and was about seven feet tall, had no arms, two webbed feet, and two green eyes." Then, it started moving toward the car. Horrified, the driver tried to turn the car around. But it was difficult to maneuver in the small space. One of the teens looked out the window. The creature was fifteen feet away! The driver wrestled the car around, and the trio zoomed back to Mansfield, bursting at the seams to share their story with someone, but feared being laughed at. On Friday, they divulged the story to one of the boy's father, who laughed at their story. He suggested if they indeed saw something, it would have left some sign of its existence—maybe tracks. They returned with the boy's father and later with a deputy from the sheriff's office. Sure enough, there were two duck-like tracks.

The Vinton County Wild Cat
Vinton County

Since the early 1900s, rumors have circulated of a huge wildcat roaming the area about ten miles south of Cedar Falls and to Vinton Furnace Experimental Station just outside McArthur. There was only one account of an attack in 1908 by a young man toting guns who had heartily provoked the beast. Since then, folks have only gotten fleeting glimpses of the critter or found large cat paw prints in the mud. It could be a released pet that got too large to keep. Or it might be the legendary Wampus Cat, a half-human and half-cat from Appalachian folklore—a witch caught in mid-spell, turning herself into a cat to sneak into a home and rob the family, then trapped between the two beings for eternity.

After moving to the county years ago, our real estate agent told us of her encounter with the legendary wildcat while evaluating property near Vinton Furnace with another agent. The two had to trek back through brush and briars for about 30 minutes dressed in high heels and skirts. Once they evaluated the property, our agent blinked, narrowed her gaze, then took in the form of a large mountain lion gazing hungrily in her direction, keeling forward and wiggling its butt.

She told me that its long tail was swishing back and forth. I eagerly interrupted her because I imagined my fat tomcat using those same movements right before it pounced on my toes as easy prey. "Holy crap, what did you do?" I asked with bated breath. "I think it was readying to eat you. You were a half-hour from your truck!" And she replied quite unassumingly, "Not on the way back, we weren't!"

Loveland Frogman
Hamilton/Clermont/ Warren County

Loveland, Ohio, is settled into the western side of Ohio, a suburb of Cincinnati described as having a small-town atmosphere with a large city feel. The Little Miami River runs through it, along with a bit of the popular seventy-mile Little Miami State Park bike trail. Over the years, Loveland has been visited by strange creatures. In 1955, a short-order cook traveled through Branch Hill on the Loveland-Madeira Pike and caught an odd sight in his headlights. Standing erect were three to four feet tall beings with leathery skin and frog faces. They held wands in their hands, waving them above their heads. Curious, he stopped, exited his car, and watched them for a few minutes before speeding away. That year, a civil defense worker witnessed the same creatures beneath a bridge as he drove past. In more recent years, a couple playing 'Pokémon Go' between Loveland Madeira Road and Lake Isabella saw such a creature stand up on two legs and come out of the water!

The creatures may be explained in history. In the 1700s, along the Little Miami, there lived Native Indians-The Miami (Mihtohseeniaki, The People), also called the Twightwee by nearby Delaware. Among those early tribes living on the Little Miami shores, a legend was passed on to French settlers of the Shawnahooc—a human-like creature with wrinkled skin and lacking a nose and living within the waters. They spoke of a party of hunters returning to their home that came across the demon-like monster, and even as they shot at it, the creature jumped into the water unharmed.

Defiance Werewolf
Defiance County

In the town of Defiance during July and August of 1972, a strange werewolf-like creature showed up along a two-block stretch of the densely populated area near the train service depot. Witnesses described the creature as 7 to 8 feet tall and very hairy. It had fangs and raggedy clothes. The police took reports believing that it was a robber, at first, and not a prankster. "Very hairy is the first description given by each person who saw the *werewolf*," Chief Breckler of the Defiance Police told reporters. "We don't think it is a prank. He's coming at people with a club in his hand—" He also relayed two brakemen working the N&W local freight serving Defiance on an overnight run—Tom Jones and Ted Davis saw the beast. They stated it "had huge hairy feet, fangs, and ran from side to side, like a caveman in the movies." They also reported it had appeared twice—both under a full moon around 4 a.m. Davis would tell the local newspaper, The Blade— "I was connecting an air hose between two cars and was looking down. I saw these huge hairy feet, then I looked up, and he was standing there with that big stick over his shoulder. When I started to say something, he took off for the woods." After that, reports started popping up all over town. A woman's doorknob rattled with the strange creature on the other side, and a grocery store employee driving home from work caught the form in his headlights at four in the morning. Others came forward who had seen the creature that appeared to be wearing dark clothing, blue jeans, and had long fangs. Then, as quickly as it appeared, it disappeared.

Melon Heads
Lake County

There was a Doctor Crowe who lived in a hidden pocket of woods near Kirtland, along Wisner Road in the 1950s. Within his care, he had orphans who suffered from hydrocephalus, a condition caused by excess fluid buildup in the brain. If left untreated, this condition hinders mental functioning, causes visual disorders, and makes it difficult to walk. He was supposed to be healing his small wards. Instead, he conducted horrible scientific experiments on them. It left the children deformed with hairless heads and their minds irrational. Many died during his procedures, but some lived. One night, they turned on the doctor and murdered him. Then, they ran into the woods, where they still live today.

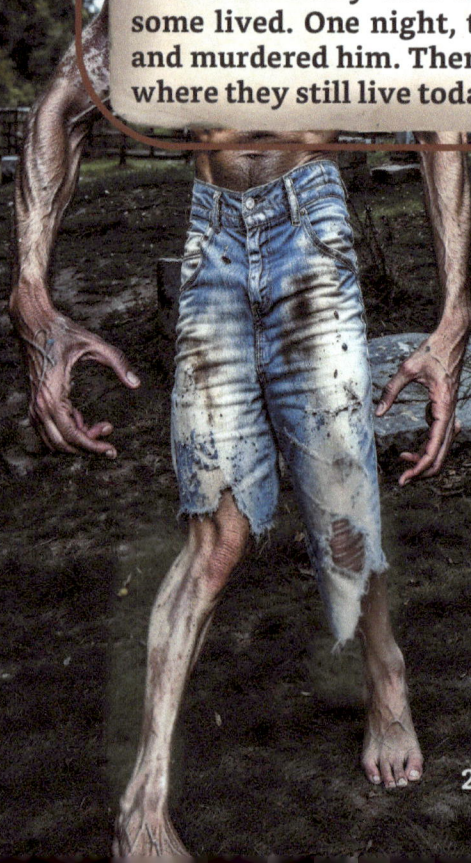

Peninsula Python
Summit County

In the summer of 1944, a monster snake slithered into the Everett swamp area of northern Ohio. It became dubbed the Peninsula Python as it made its circuit through the communities. Clarence Mitchell saw it in his cornfield. He told a Cleveland Press reporter: "I don't know what made me look up, but there, about fifteen paces away, was the biggest snake I ever seen, sliding along easy and slow in plain sight on the bare ground. I just stood quiet, not aiming to attract attention. It seemed like ten minutes I watched. He slid into the river, swam across, and climbed out the other side. He was as thick as my thigh, right here, and every bit of fifteen feet long—more like eighteen—sort of brownish spotted. I went over and looked at the track. It was like you'd rolled a spare tire across my field." The next day, Missus Vaughn watched it eat one of her chickens whole. A woman living on Brandywine-Hudson Road milking her cows noted they were unusually nervous. She looked at a dead willow tree near the river and watched a snake's head as big as a man's head slip out of the limbs. It caused a wild goose chase by police across the countryside as more witnesses came forward before the snake slithered back into obscurity. Most attributed the python's existence to a circus truck wreck. In June of 1942, a King Brothers Circus truck filled with tent canvas went out of control on a steep hill. It crashed into the nearby Ira Cemetery and into the headstones, overturning. The driver was killed. Some believe that there were more than just tents in the truck.

South Bay Bessie
Lorain/Huron/Sandusky, Ottawa/Erie County

In northern Ohio, Lake Erie is shallow and warm for such a vast expanse of water. Home to plenty of freshwater fish, it has become the perfect habitat for a giant serpent-like creature lurking in the depths whose first sightings were recorded in 1793. The captain of the Felicity came across a sixteen-foot creature while hunting ducks near Sandusky, Ohio. Then, in May of 1897, it reared its head above the water near the Pelee Island Lighthouse high enough that the lightkeeper, William Grubb saw it.

In the 1980s, Theresa Kovach was one of two women who saw the creature playing among the waves. She believed it was large enough to capsize a boat and described it as having big flippers, reptilian and snake-like. In 1990, Dennis Szececinski of Toledo reported seeing the sea monster when fishing—described as long and black slithering in Maumee Bay near Toledo's water intake structure. The same month, Harold Bricker, age 67, told Ohio State Park Rangers that he and his family were fishing north of Cedar Point Amusement Park. A 30-foot serpent with a snake-like head swam by their boat.

Some cryptozoologists explain its existence as a surviving relative of the long-necked and extinct marine reptile, the Plesiosaur. This sea serpent has been described mainly as dark green or brown with a snake-like head, thirty to forty feet long, and appearing to undulate while it swims in the deep water.

Mothman of Gallipolis
Gallia County

Gallipolis was just a quiet Ohio River community connected to Point Pleasant, West Virginia, by a long, steel bridge when life there was disrupted by a strange man-like flying creature that visited in November of 1966. It started with five men digging a grave across the river in Clendenin, witnessing what they were sure was a man flying over their heads.

Near Point Pleasant, two couples were chased in their car along a remote wooded roadway by a sizeable white apparition with glowing eyes in the area that would later be known as the lair of the creature, the McClintic Wildlife Management Area, an old TNT plant. There were several UFO sightings over Gallipolis when the Mothman held the reign of terror along the river. Mysterious "Men in Black" showed up, frightening many from talking about the event. Then, on December 15, 1967, 46 people died as the bridge that connected Point Pleasant, West Virginia, and Gallipolis, Ohio collapsed. Some believe that the Mothman prophesied the disaster. But nobody has ever figured out why the Men in Black arrived at the same time.

Crosswick Monster
Warren County

Crosswick is a small community just a few miles from Caesar Creek State Park. In May of 1882, a strange story arose of two boys, 9-year-old Joe and 14-year-old Ed Lynch, who set out to fish at a small creek, Satterthwaites Run, south of their home. They stopped along the bank and set up poles, commencing right away to fish. It was not long before they heard a scratching sound of reeds and brush moving and to their horror, a huge lizard-like monster rushed toward them.

It was ten times their size, with legs as tall as the oldest boy, and dragged a black and white tail covered with yellow spots. A forked tongue popped out and the boys screamed. The sound awakened something in the monster and it reached out two clawed arms and snatched the elder of the two boys in its grasp, dragging him to a big sycamore with a hollow base and a hole in the side where it thrust him inside. The boy's wails caught the attention of three men who were quarrying stone not far away and they along with a crowd gathered began to cut the tree down. The lizard jumped out and escaped into the brush and was never found. Although the young boy was bruised, he did live.

Witnesses still saw the strange monster at the Little Miami River for years. Farms in the area did have missing animals attributed to the creature. In 1978, a couple at nearby Caesar Creek State Park even witnessed a creature not unlike the Crosswick monster.

Octoman
Clermont County

In January of 1959, more than a few believable witnesses started reporting a strange, almost indescribable creature rising from the waters and bobbing playfully in the Ohio and Little Miami Rivers. Dispatchers thought it was a hoax until they got more calls, one including a truck driver heading down OH-125 who told them, "It came up out of the water. I can't describe it, and I have never seen anything like it before. All I want to do is get out of here and on to Indianapolis."

Another man said he was driving along, and something hopped onto the bridge. "It was large, not a dog or cat. It leaped in front of my car and, on two legs, was taller than my auto. When I looked back in my mirror, it was moving along the bridge rail." He described the creature as three to four times the size of a man and much bulkier. Another woman described it as appearing like an octopus bobbing above the water. The massive entity with pale green skin that was also depicted as having rolls of fat came and went. Strangely there was a power outage at about the same time it visited.

Ohio River Monster
Hamilton County

On Friday, January 11th, 1878, Ben Karrick saw a sea serpent in the Ohio River beneath the Roebling Suspension Bridge, where his delivery wagon was working its way across. It was twelve to fifteen feet long and had the head of an enormous serpent. A black glossy substance like hair covered the body, and the skin was like the rugged hide of an alligator. It lashed its tail several times and moved fast, hissing and making a deep bellow, much like a cow's low. He compared it to a colossal seahorse. It must have been making its way along the river as only a day earlier, the mast of the steamboat Silver Moon, when docked, saw a creature of its exact likeness. Fifteen years later, travelers near Blennerhassett Island were stunned to see a massive sea serpent, ten feet long with an immense head and bulbous eyes, drifting up to their boat.

Devil Monkey
Lawrence County

In 1875, workers and foot travelers around the Vesuvius iron furnace were waylaid by a baboon-like creature with a long black tail and short legs. In March of 1875, a man from Long Creek was running along State Route 141, taking the long way home past Vesuvius Iron Furnace. He heard thrashing in some bushes. A thickly built creature with squatty legs and a long tail burst into his path. As quickly as the beast appeared, it disappeared. Those who saw it called the creature a devil monkey.

It is obviously still around; about midnight on a balmy June 26th, 1997, in Dunkinsville, Ohio, a woman saw a hairy animal with a tail, three to four feet tall, walking on its back legs and using its knuckles to help propel it forward.

Little Green Men
Greene County

Wright-Patterson Air Force Base is located northeast of Dayton, Ohio. There has always been chatter about aliens at that particular Air Force base hidden in a storage freezer in a secret bunker. They are the bodies recovered from the famous crash site in Roswell, New Mexico, in 1947. Those who saw them moved there said they were tiny and gray, about four feet tall, with big pear-shaped heads and slanted eyes.

Some say the crash never happened at all, that it was just a test balloon. Others disagree, including the Air Force, which denies the rumors. Everyone has a theory, many quite different. However, it is hard not to believe looking up at the sky that just goes on and on and on. Historic newspapers are filled with articles and reports of UFO (Unidentified Flying Objects) sightings from Cincinnati to Cleveland farther back than the 1950s. Ohio has even been called a hotbed for activity. It doesn't matter if those aliens are frozen solid in that lab. *Something* is out there. It is just a matter of time before we know what it is.